Dog in School

story by Jeremy Strong
illustrated by Steve Smallman

Sam was on her way to school.
She took the lift down to the ground floor.
When the doors opened she got
a surprise.

A dog was standing outside the lift.
It had a fluffy coat with black and
brown markings.
It had big, floppy ears.

"What are you doing here?" said Sam.

The dog had no name tag on its collar.

"You are a mystery dog," said Sam.

"Woof!" barked the dog and wagged its tail.

Sam set off for school and the dog
followed her.

"Go home. You can't come with me,"
laughed Sam.

On the way she met Ben and the twins.

The dog jumped up to lick them.
"Who is this?" asked Mouse.
"Has it got a name?"
"I am going to call him Mystery,"
said Sam. "I wish he was mine."

Mystery followed them to school.
They shut the gate so that the dog
could not get in.
"Goodbye," said Sam sadly.
"Woof!" barked the dog.

The children went to their classroom.

Mr Hopkins began to call out their names.

"Sam Summerday," he called.

"Woof!"

Everyone turned to look.

The dog was outside the window.

"There's a dog in school,"
the children shouted.
"Stay here," said Mr Hopkins.
"We cannot have a dog in school.
I will go and catch it."

Mr Hopkins went outside.
Mystery ran away.
Mr Hopkins ran after the
dog and Mystery ran faster.

"We must help," said Sam,
and she ran outside.
The rest of the class went with her.

Mr Hopkins chased the dog round
and round the playground.

The children chased the dog round
and round the playground.
"Woof! Woof!" barked Mystery happily.

The headteacher, Mrs Turner, came out.
"What is all this noise about?" she said.
The dog ran between her legs
and into the school.
"Oh!" cried Mrs Turner.

The dog ran from one classroom
to another, barking and jumping
and wagging its tail.

The teachers chased the dog.
The children chased the dog.

Even the school cook ran after the dog.
"Come here!" they all cried.

At last Mystery ran into a cupboard.
Mr Hopkins slammed the door.
"There! We have caught the dog. Phew!"
He wiped his face with a big hanky.

There was a lot of banging and
barking from inside the cupboard.
Mrs Turner got a skipping rope.
"Open the door a bit. I will use this
rope as a lead."

Mr Hopkins opened the door.
Mrs Turner tied the rope
to the dog's collar.
"It is all right now."
smiled Mrs Turner.

But when Mr Hopkins opened the
door wide they saw a terrible mess!
The dog had upset all the paint.
It wasn't black and brown any more.
He was red and blue and green
and yellow!

"I have seen this dog at the pub,"
said Mrs Turner. "I will take it back
at lunch time."
"Can I come with you?" asked Sam.
"The dog followed me to school.
I would like to help you take him back."

Mrs Turner let Sam hold the rope.

The people at the pub were glad to get their dog back.

"We were looking for him," they said.

"What is his name?" asked Sam.

"I called him Mystery."

"Oh no! He isn't called Mystery. His name is Trouble!"